Titles by Janvier Chouteu-Chando

The Usurper: and Other Stories
Triple Agent, Double Cross
Disciples of Fortune
The Union Moujik
Splendid Comets
Flash of the Sun
Fortune Calls
Fortune's Master
Fortune's Children
The Norilsk Bears
To Be In Love and To Be Wise
The Fire and Ice Legend
The Sweetest Madness
The Grandmothers
The Hunger Fire
The Shades of Fire
Father and Sons
The Doctors
Dark Shades
Fateful Ties
The Verdict of Hades
His Majesty's Trial
Ngoko's Folly
The Usurper
The Dowry
I am Hated
The Oaf

Non-Fiction Titles by Janvier Chouteu-Chando

THEIR LAST STAND: Donald Trump's Upset Victory…
BROKEN ENGAGEMENT: Why a Donald Trump Win…
Ukraine: The Tug-of-war between Russia and the West
Cameroon: The Haunted Heart of Africa

Who the Enemies of the People are, and How They are Fighting Against Change: and Others

Janvier Tchouteu

TISI BOOKS

NEW YORK, RALEIGH, LONDON, AMSTERDAM

PUBLISHED BY TISI BOOKS
www.tisibooks.com

PUBLISHED BY TISI BOOKS
www.tisibooks.com

NEW YORK, RALEIGH, LONDON, AMSTERDAM

Printed in The United States of America

EPIGRAPH

"The time for revolutionaries with the complete freedom to maneuver is over."
—CHRISTOPHER NKWAYEP-CHANDO

Acknowledgement

My deepest, warmest and everlasting thanks to Dr. Samuel F. Tchwenko and Christopher N. Chando for challenging me towards the path of humanity's enhancement.

DEDICATION

Dedicated to the loving memory of Salomon Muna Yakana

Who the Enemies of the People are, and How They are Fighting Against Change: and Others

Contents

Quotes

"Cameroon is not a country of slaves that no man can free."
Janvier Chouteu-Chando

"Every great cause begins as a movement, becomes a business, and eventually degenerates into a racket."
Eric Hoffer

"We are not involved in this struggle only because we think that we will dismantle this system in the course of our life. We hope Cameroon changes tomorrow. But if it doesn't, we will be happy to know that we made the ground fertile for the next generation that will end the rot in this country, and then establish the "NEW CAMEROON".
Dr. Samuel F. Tchwenko, former UPCist and chief ideologue of the historic SDF of 1990-2002

"The enemy is not the one who is facing you with a sword in hand, that's the opponent. The enemy is the one behind you with a knife at your back."
Thomas Sankara

"However [political parties] may now and then answer popular ends, they are likely in the course of time and things, to become potent engines, by which cunning, ambitious, and unprincipled men will be enabled to subvert the power of the people and to usurp for themselves the reins of government, destroying afterwards the very engines which have lifted them to unjust dominion."
George Washington

"We know that Africa is neither French, nor British, nor American, nor Russian, that it is African. We know the objects of the West. Yesterday they divided us on the level of a tribe, clan and village...They want to create antagonistic blocs, satellites..."

Patrice Lumumba

"You see these dictators on their pedestals, surrounded by the bayonets of their soldiers and the truncheons of their police ... yet in their hearts there is unspoken fear. They are afraid of words and thoughts: words spoken abroad, thoughts stirring at home -- all the more powerful because forbidden -- terrify them. A little mouse of thought appears in the room, and even the mightiest potentates are thrown into panic."

Winston S. Churchill

"...The world gets blessed every now and then with unique souls who though burdened by their invisible crosses, still have the extraordinary strength to forge ahead in life and give others a helping hand at the same time. Despite their tribulations, most of us think they are fine. Even when the weight of their crosses become unbearable, even when they proceed in a breathless manner, we still have a hard time understanding that they are drowning. In fact, we even condemn them for failing to sacrifice more..."

Janvier Chouteu-Chando, Disciples of Fortune

"The greatest difficulty we have faced is the neocolonial way of thinking that exists in this country. We were colonized by a country, France, that left us with certain habits. For us, being successful in life, being happy, meant trying to live as they do in France, like the richest of the French."

Thomas Sankara

"Loyalty to country ALWAYS. Loyalty to government, when it deserves it."
<u>**Mark Twain**</u>

"A minimum of comfort is necessary for the practice of virtue."
Patrice Lumumba

"They wrote in the old days that it is sweet and fitting to die for one's country. But in modern war, there is nothing sweet nor fitting in your dying. You will die like a dog for no good reason."
<u>**Ernest Hemingway**</u>

"We find that at present the human race is divided into one wise man, nine knaves, and ninety fools out of every hundred. That is, by an optimistic observer. The nine knaves assemble themselves under the banner of the most knavish among them, and become 'politicians'; the wise man stands out, because he knows himself to be hopelessly outnumbered, and devotes himself to poetry, mathematics, or philosophy; while the ninety fools plod off under the banners of the nine villains, according to fancy, into the labyrinths of chicanery, malice and warfare. It is pleasant to have command, observes Sancho Panza, even over a flock of sheep, and that is why the politicians raise their banners. It is, moreover, the same thing for the sheep whatever the banner. If it is democracy, then the nine knaves will become members of parliament; if fascism, they will become party leaders; if communism, commissars. Nothing will be different, except the name. The fools will be still fools, the knaves still leaders, the results still exploitation. As for the wise man, his lot will be much the same under any ideology. Under democracy he will be encouraged to starve to death in a garret, under fascism he will be put in a concentration camp, under communism he will be liquidated."

T.H. White

INTRODUCTION

The cause for change being pursued today by the majority of Cameroonians (the struggling masses) does not bear its origins from the wind of change (demands for democracy) that Soviet leader Mikhail Sergeivich Gorbachev's Glasnost and Perestroika generated across the world, a wind of change that jolted those political systems that were failing to conform to the demands of world civilization and progress, which place the freedom and liberty of man and the interest of humanity above the twisted interest of the unscrupulous selfish minority.

The cause for change otherwise known as the Cameroonian (Kamerunian) Struggle began in 1910 led by Martin Paul Samba (Mebene Mebongo). Patriotic Cameroonians, who accept one another irrespective of their compatriots' ethnic, racial, religious or regional origins, acknowledge the fact that the first phase of the Kamerunian (Cameroonian) struggle was defeated in 1914 by the German colonial army following the execution of Martin Paul Samba and Rudolf Duala Manga Bell. They also accept the fact that because of that defeat, the land lost a unifying patriotic or civic-nationalist force to ensure Kamerun's unity during and after the First World War (The Great War), a void that played against the Kamerunian people when the victorious British and French colonial powers went about partitioning the defeated German Kamerun after the war.

The lethargy that followed the first defeat of the

Kamerunian struggle and the resultant partition of the pre-1911 German Kamerun into French Cameroun and British Cameroons (British Northern Cameroons and British Southern Cameroons) lasted for thirty years, or the equivalent of a generation, before the divided Kamerunian people revived their national consciousness again. This time around, the revival of the original objectives of the Kamerunian struggle—independence, freedom, justice, development, unity, peace, democracy, liberty, progress, international cooperation and international fraternity—was done with an additional objective of reuniting a land and a people who through no fault of theirs had been separated from one another to suit the interest of Britain, France and other foreign powers.

Reuniting Kamerunians also meant mitigating the consequences of partition and putting the land and its people on the path to realize the original purpose of the Kamerunian struggle embodied in the words "THE KAMERUNIAN DREAM" (CAMEROONIAN DREAM). This second phase of the Kamerunian struggle dominated by the quest for reunification of British Cameroons and French Cameroun was led by the UPC (*Union des Populations du Cameroun"*, otherwise known as the Union of the Populations of the Cameroons), a legal political party born in French Cameroun on April 11, 1948. The UPC and its affiliate political parties commanded more than 90% of the support of educated Cameroonians in both French Cameroun and British Cameroons and had the open or tacit backing or sympathy of more than 80% of British Cameroonians and French Camerounians before the vindictive and fearful French authorities banned the UPC on July 13, 1955, a move that was backed two years later by the British authorities in British Cameroons when the authorities there also banned the UPC in 1957. With the elimination from the political scene of the party that was the land's most dominant movement and that was the best reflection of the aspirations of the Cameroonian people, advocates for reunification and independence for the lands of the former German Kamerun(British Cameroons &French Cameroun) were in a predicament.

The fact that the UPC was left after its ban with no other option to freely lead the struggling "Kamerunian Masses" to their aspirations, the fact that the colonial powers perceived the UPC as an obstacle in their design and influence over the former German Kamerun, and the fact that its members were being hounded and killed, the UPC finally came to a conclusion that it had no other option but to resort to the path of armed resistance. The painful decision that led to more than ten years of armed resistance contributed enormously in the political evolution of the territories of the former German Kamerun and the partial reunification of these territories (British Southern Cameroons and French Cameroun), but it came about with the death of more than half a million Cameroonians (10% of the population), and it came about with the loss of British Northern Cameroons to Nigeria. Yes, the cause that spurred the fight for Cameroon's reunification and independence resulted in the reunification of British Southern Cameroons and the Republic of Cameroon (the former French Cameroon) in 1961, following the plebiscite results in British Southern Cameroons, but the price paid in achieving that was very high indeed—Cameroonians witnessed the first case of crimes against humanity committed by the French Army in French Cameroun and the puppet regime they put in place there after they made French Cameroun a member of the United Nations Organization on January 01, 1960 by granting it independence in a process that effectively made the territory a neocolonial possession of France.

The assassination of the Ruben Um Nyobe (The UPC's leader) on 13 September 1958 by French forces; the poisoning of his successor Felix-Roland Moumié in Geneva in October 1960 by the William Bechtel, an agent of the French secret service; and the execution of the third historic UPC leader Ernest Ouandié in January 15, 1971, after he gave himself up in August 1970; marked the second defeat of the Kamerunian struggle, the successful entrenchment of the French-imposed system under the regime of French puppet Ahmadou Ahidjo (the first Cameroonian president), and a new reality of a pseudo-independence to soothe the pains and emotions of the patriotic struggling Cameroonian masses and to neutralize their civic-nationalism, a very peculiar union-nationalism also called Kamerunism, which is considered an advanced ideal that brings diverse peoples together in a continent plagued by ethnic, religious and racial divisions. The carrot and stick strategy of suppression, intimidation, handouts, extortion, bribery and corruption that the French political leadership under the umbrella of FrancAfrique (France's special relationship with its former African colonies and territories established before it granted them independence) sustained the 24-year rule of Ahmadou Ahidjo, and has been sustaining the usurper regime of Ahidjo's successor Paul Biya ever since he was handed power by Ahmadou Ahidjo in 1982.

That defeat of the second phase of the Cameroonian struggle led to a second political lethargy that even saw the democratic nature of the former British Cameroons undermined after Cameroon's reunification, a process of subjugation that kept the dynamic Cameroonian people docile or politically subdued for two decades.

Today, we are in the third and hopefully or certainly the last phase of the Cameroonian Struggle to realize the Kamerunian Dream of "THE NEW CAMEROON".

That the struggling Cameroonian masses have been whisked off their political lethargy is glaring for all to see; that their determination to realize the objectives of the eight-decade old Kamerunian(Cameroonian) struggle is clearly and resolutely challenged or resisted by the status quo or the Biya regime and its external backers (The French- politically setup in Africa otherwise known as FrancAfrique) that have been benefitting from the mafia setup called the Cameroonian system, is something the world knows about. But exponents of change in Cameroon know that getting rid of the anachronistic French-imposed system is the only recourse which would allow Cameroonians to build "The New Cameroon" that would involve Cameroonians of all ethnic groups, religions, political affiliations, regions and races in the process of nation-building. Cameroonians know that getting rid of the system is the first step in reconciling Cameroon and Cameroonians.

In power since 1982 is Africa's absentee dictator Paul Biya, who was made the successor of his predecessor Ahmadou Ahidjo by an order from former French President Francoise Mitterrand; Ahidjo, who himself was brought to power by the French to usurp the aspirations of Cameroonians in their liberation struggle led by the UPC that the French banned in 1955, a party with more than 80% of the land's intellectuals and even more national support. France had made sure Ahidjo's power was secured by decimating its support base in a 12-year war against the party and by killing all the UPC leaders (Un Nyobe 1958, Felix Moumie in Geneva 1960, Ossende Ofana 1966, Ernest Ouandie 1971 etc.), leaving Cameroon a nation haunted by an "Unfinished Liberation Struggle". Today, Cameroonians are out not only to get rid of the Dictator Biya's autocracy, but also to get rid of the French-imposed system that its custodians want to continue with someone else after Paul Biya departs.

Chapter One

*Who the Enemies of the People are, and
How They are Fighting Against Change*

The vast majority of the Cameroonian people are aware of the historical revelation that change is inevitable in Cameroon. Still, this craving for change since 1910 has not brought about the realization of the New Cameroon. We have all been victims in this difficult, tortuous, traitorous and unsuccessful drive for change. The execution of our first nationalist leaders (Martin Paul Samba and Rudolf Duala Manga Bell) by the German colonial army in 1914, our indifference over that loss, our quiet acceptance of the partition of German Kamerun by Britain and France into British Cameroons and French Cameroun, and the methodical suppression and brainwashing of our nationalism were all indications of the difficulties ahead for the Cameroonian struggle.

Yes, we were in a state o f lethargy for three decades after partition, a lethargy that left us without the enthusiasm and an organized force to repudiate the imposed partition of our land and realize our resurgent nationalism in both British Cameroons and French Cameroun. This nationalism assumed a union character by advocating for reunification, independence, freedom, liberty, development of both territories. Yet, it was a popular desire for change fraught with division, the self-centeredness of uncommitted leaders and external maneuvers by the colonial powers. The outcome of that second phase of the Cameroonian struggle was a partially reunited and quasi-independent Cameroon, where its French-speaking union-nationalist leaders got eliminated, exiled or subjugated; where its English-speaking union-nationalists were excluded and cowed into timidity; and where a Neo-colonialists French-imposed system was put in place managed in Cameroon by the regimes of puppets Ahmadou Ahidjo and Paul Biya.

The first Cameroonian president, his collaborators and French masters had little or no knowledge of and regard for the true aspirations of the Cameroonian people. Therefore, in no way could we have expected the Ahidjo regime and its successor the Biya regime to deliver Cameroonians to the change that they have been craving for since 1910. It is clear that the foundation of the quasi-independent and reunited Cameroon was defective even before the nation was born in 1961. Cameroon's independence was defective because it was realized under the usurper Ahidjo regime and France without the consent of the majority of Cameroonians who constitute the force of our union-nationalism.

If the usurper leaders could not kill in themselves all the values, thought patterns and habits imbued by their French overlords, then how could we have expected them to lead Cameroonians to live the values and pattern of change that would lead to the new and desirable society of our dreams. This land has never had its destiny in its own hands since it became a consolidated entity. Imperialistic French designs in the guise of the French-imposed system, the complicity of the Ahidjo and Biya regimes, and the unpatriotic, unscrupulous and smug complacent nature of some Cameroonians have all contributed to cloud the Cameroonian dream for an authentic change (the creation of the desirable society) and the realization of the New Cameroon. The demanding task of freeing ourselves from the shackles of the Biya dictatorship, the retarding French-imposed system and the suffocation of the people with the evil disposition is not going to be easy. That task requires the best combination of reasoning, enthusiasm and rational desire. It is our shortcomings in our concerted efforts at interpreting, manifesting and applying those forces that are affecting the wind of change in Cameroon today.

May 26, 1990, marked a turning point in the history of the reunified Cameroon. The corrupt, oppressive, discriminatory, nonchalant, unpatriotic and incompetent rule of the Ahidjo-Biya regimes under the French-imposed oligarchic system became opposed across the national territory. Cameroonians were determined to become a part of the worldwide wind of change generated by Mikhail Gorbachev's policy of Glasnost and Perestroika in the Soviet Union.

"Enough is enough", *"We want democracy, freedom, and liberty"*, were some of the chants that illuminated the protest marches across the national territory.

Cameroonians were no longer prepared to continue allowing a nepotistic, ethnocentric, oligarchic, corrupt and neo-colonialist system under the Biya regime and its French backers to determine the course of our destiny. We were vocal in our determination to stop allowing the weight of decades of oppression, misinformation and misguided policies to drain us of our dynamism and deprive us from realizing our century-old dream of a progressive Cameroon. Our expressed desire for change was a popular aspiration, which called on Cameroonians to discard the wrong aspects of our past and build a new, totally and completely positive Cameroon. Our vocal determination not to be left behind in the worldwide wind of change that promised to realize a free society of nations was understood across Africa and the rest of the world. Five years after we took that historic step in the third phase of the Cameroon struggle, we are nowhere close to the change or the power that is the lever to realize it. Our potentially great nation is being left behind in the race to technological civilization and the trappings of human and material progress due to the steadfastness of the anti-people system. However, what is most worrying is that, at this early stage of the struggle, the forces for change are more divided than they were before 1990.

What went wrong?

Five years after, it has become clear for all to see that we have betrayed the drive towards change. We wanted change without ensuring a fundamental change of our mentalities, which had been badly infected during the years of political lethargy. Yes, we wanted change when we had not humanized our dehumanized selves. The change we wanted was only in words. We failed to react, respond and feel to the new demands of change as a renewed and reinvigorated people. That is why we could not detach ourselves from the more blinding aspects of our irrational desires, in order to conform to reasoning and enthusiasm. We have not fully braced ourselves to throw away the influences of the past years of colonialism, political lethargy, despondence, dishonesty, cynicism and distrust that had gripped the noble Cameroonian soul. Our desire for change has almost been defeated by the open and hidden enemies of change because of our empty phrases, feeble actions and divided ranks. The enemies of the people have pervaded our midst, ebbed away our energy and actions, denigrated our objectives and poisoned our minds. The enemies of the people have left Cameroonians, even those who are instinctively union-nationalist, in disarray

But then, who are these enemies of the people?

Simply, they are the criminals to the progressive Cameroonian spirit, the obstacles to the realization of the century old Cameroonian dream for a desirable society. Amongst the enemies of the people are the anti-union-nationalists, the pseudo-intellectuals, the unscrupulous politicians, the verminous businesspersons, the oblivious functionaries, neurotic leaders and even we the struggling masses.

1) The anti-union-nationalists, also made up of pseudo-nationalists, can be found in and out of the government of Paul Biya. These anti-union-nationalists are against the century old Cameroonian dream— an advanced ideal permeated by progressive Cameroonian concepts that is aimed at:

- Creating a genuine bilingual character for the nation
- Bridging the gap in the development of both the English and French-speaking territories
- Realizing a new, desirable and humanized Cameroonian mentality from the different breeds of thoughts and actions of its Anglophone and Francophone children

2) The pseudo-intellectuals are anti-union-nationalist with the extra cloak of advanced learning. The fact that they are detached from the Cameroonian dream subjects their high learning to misuse. These pseudo-intellectuals defend the shortcomings of their personal, family, clique, ethnic, linguistic and cultural attachments to the system through unjustifiable lies that defame the cause. Found at all levels in the Cameroonian society, they easily ally with both the internal and external forces against the people. They dominate the present regime, and they are noted for their failure to make their high learning compatible with the Cameroonian reality and to contribute to Cameroon's

socio-economic progress. They have never interpreted ideas, conveyed opinions and worked for the true aspirations of the people during the past four decades. These pseudo-intellectuals led by Paul-Biya are the greatest junks to the practical progress of this nation. They have distinguished themselves as those who have been spectacular in one field, but who for the sake of publicity and self-interest, expound beyond the limits of their talents and knowledge, and seek to educate, convince and win over the uninformed and undecided on subjects far beyond their scope. While engaging in this deception, these pseudo-intellectuals are aware of the fact that some people believe and respect them as intellectuals due to their academic achievements and ratings in their true fields. The fact that they go ahead to expound on the fields much beyond their scope and grasp, while knowing that they know little, and while also knowing that the people do not know that they know little beyond their true fields, makes them criminals to the progressive Cameroonian spirit. During the past four decades, the anti-union-nationalists have been working with the pseudo-intellectuals and the French powerhouse to give Cameroonians a false concept of themselves and to derail and delay the fundamental changes that we have been craving for.

3) Cameroonian politicians manifest the inner contradictions that have gripped our political scene during the past five decades. It has been observed with clarity that our politics is mostly a juxtaposition of anti-francophone

practices, anti-Anglophone tendencies, ethnocentrism, regionalism, elitism, demagoguery and self-interest. Few of our political leaders are union-nationalists at heart even though the Cameroonian spirit is instinctively proud of the Cameroonian identity and upholds the dream of a desirable Cameroonian society. The different politicians and political groupings are very much a reflection of the extent of their embracement of these contradictory values. All the same, few of our politicians have indicated their true positions over the different concepts. Many insincerely identify themselves with popular political groupings whose ideologies they do not share. A look at these politicians can give us insights into the dilemma union-nationalists are facing in the struggle.

- The Francophiles or Anglophobes are those politicians who have an excessive fondness of French values, customs, people, institutions and/or manners. In their over-zealousness, they jealously or regretfully defend their fondness for anything French by being Anglophobes in rhetoric and actions. Besides being Francophiles, these politicians are openly ethnocentric, nepotistic and self-centered. It is clear for all to see that Francophiles have overwhelming dominated the system through the Ahidjo and Biya regimes.

- The counterparts of the Francophiles are the Anglophiles or Francophobes. They also share the ethnocentric, nepotistic and self-centeredness of the Francophiles. They have been very much excluded from the country's political life just as much as the union-nationalists have. But many of them hide or have hidden their anti-French tendencies for the benefits and opportunities offered by the French-imposed system. The fact that these Francophiles and Anglophiles have snuggled themselves into all the major political groupings makes it difficult for the realization of change because they pose as the major dividing force in the country. In the most unfortunate accident in our history, Cameroon has been dominated by the minority regimes of Francophiles and their Anglophone collaborators. Time has proven that this nightmarish alliance and governance led to the ruination of our country to the pathetic state that it is today. All true union-nationalists need to take upon themselves the responsibilities to mitigate the effects of the bitterness and the distrust that exists between some in our English and French-speaking communities.

- An insult to the progressive minds of Cameroonians are the group of politicians whose political parties are out to secure individual, tribal or group interest— politicians who openly flaunt their disregard for the collective Cameroonian interest. The MDR of Diakolle Diasalla, the renegade UPC of Augustine Kodock, the PDC, etc. dominate this group.

- Cameroonians are also aware of another ambiguous group of politicians who have also snuggled themselves into popular political groups that have a national character and are regarded as the true guarantors of change. These so-called friends of the people are the most heinous of Judases who have concealed their vast selfish designs and traits of Francophilism, Anglophilism, tribalism, ethnocentrism and regionalism behind the general phrase of working for the interest of the people. Scratch them and you will find the enemies of the people, their true selves, staring back at you. However, their impatience and the goodwill of nature shall soon force them out of the mainstream of the struggle.

The people whose dreams have been betrayed and whose enthusiasm and dignity have been undermined should know that unless these pillars of reaction, conservatism and deceit are overthrown or rendered impotent, we would always find ourselves held back in our genuine efforts for change. It should be understood that these forces against change would persist in their deceptive ways in order to maintain their selfish interests and biased motives. Their steadfastness is making it difficult for the struggling Cameroonian masses to overcome their oppression and trauma, forcing them to make only desperate, unintelligent and futile protests and resistances. The interest of Cameroonians would be guaranteed only in a situation where they stay totally committed in their support for the authentic union-nationalists who are the true friends of the people.

4) Another enemies of the people are the unscrupulous businesspersons whose game plan is to prevail economically through unlawful means. They make excessive profits through tax evasion, extortion, defrauding, profiteering, racketeering, double-dealing and complicity in the wanton destruction and sale of the country's resources. These unscrupulous businesspersons are indifferent to the fact that they are running the country down. The fact that they are in alliance with the unscrupulous Biya regime and that they dread any change that would require them to do clean business makes them enemies of the cause for a New Cameroon. Most of their cash is stashed in foreign banks because they fear the inevitable change would lead to confiscation. A critical look at the activities of the unscrupulous businesspersons reveals that they drain rather than contribute to the economy of Cameroon. They should be discouraged or legally disabled if they reject doing business in a clean manner in the New Cameroon. They are scum to the progressive business spirit, and they pose as a major obstacle to change and modernization. It should be noted that they are setting a bad precedence to the humanized and progressive businesspersons who would emerge from the new system that would emerge from change, businesspersons whose economic activities would also be

out to alleviate the standards of the Cameroonian people.

5) No less a powerful obstacle to change is the functionary. For forty years, it has been so easy for radical nationalists, intellectuals, honest managers and competent administrators to be transformed into government functionaries who console themselves with the thought that they are working for the people and doing well within the framework of office routine in the corrupt system. They are using this professed goodness to justify their political inertia and compliance with the policies of the Biya-regime. The fact that these functionaries have given their unconditional allegiance to the French-imposed system and the Biya regime makes it difficult for them to wrestle their much-deserved interest from the government. This self-created difficulty emanates from the simple fact that these functionaries always believed that a holy alliance exists between them and the regimes, an alliance where they would have to defend the system even though it had become irredeemably bad. Even though it is obvious that the Biya regime has unilaterally broken the alliance, these functionaries are still in political inertia. Because they too have been enemies of the people in their actions and opponents of change in their bygone interests, they now find it difficult to heed the general call for change and join the people from whose ranks they come from. This timidity and foolish pride from the functionaries only helps to stall the wind of change, despite the fact that reality calls for an alliance between them and the people.

6) Leadership problems have been Cameroon's infantile malady since reunification and independence. The fact that its genuine leaders who had the support of its people were massacred, exiled, sidelined and cowed into submission by the French and the puppet Ahidjo and Biya regimes left us with the curse of false leaders. Yes, the past four decades have indicated that. The leadership spectrum in Cameroon is a conflict of four types of leaders:

- We have the bad leaders whose leaderships have done much to destroy the way of life and the progressive values of the Cameroonian people. The usurper Paul Biya who presides as the president of Cameroon is a bad leader in the classic sense of the word, and rivals his predecessor in that domain. Lesser bad leaders are comic Cameroonian political figures like Augustine Kodock, Gustav Esaka, Diakolle Diasala, Achidi Achu and Bello Bouba Miagari.

- Also dominant in Cameroon's political scene are the brilliant leaders. These leaders made themselves appealing to the people even despite their true intentions and convictions. They are the demagogues and renegades to the ideals they associate with. Towering in this group are figures like Ahidjo, Solomon Tandeng Muna, Mayi Matip, Hogbe Nleng, Musonge Peter, Woungly Masaga and other noisy but insignificant political figures around. Less conspicuous are the renegades of the people's parties who are posing as union-nationalists.

- Not absent in the political game are the intelligent political figures. They get over the people and their values, and defy their beliefs through political maneuvers that only serve their interest. The intelligent leaders make the people to think, look and work in the direction that is to his interest, ego and conviction, sometimes combining his efforts with handouts and other inauthentic benevolent gestures. It is unfortunate that many Cameroonians have been brainwashed to cherish these handouts. Ahidjo and his disciples led by Bello Bouba Maigari are the masters of this deception.

- What Cameroon has been deprived of the most are the wise leaders. These are leaders who are realistic in their dealings with the people. They understand the people's plights, hopes, fears, strengths, weaknesses, and try to help them to realize their dreams. These are the true friends of the people, the true union-nationalists from the times of Martin Paul Samba to the generations of the historic UPC leaders and over to our contemporary times. Unfortunately, for the Cameroonian struggle, none of the wise leaders have ever been allowed to harness the support of the majority of Cameroonians to lead the country. We hold the French puppeteers and the puppet regimes of Ahidjo and Biya responsible for that.

7) Depressing as it may sound, another set of enemies of the people is the self-centered flag bearers. These are the Cameroonian artists, players, writers, scientists and representatives of the country abroad who in the quest for glory conceal the plight of the Cameroonian people behind the façade of success. They would not stand by the people if it means working against their interests at home and abroad.

8) To be honest with ourselves, we the struggling masses are also posing as an obstacle to change. We have desired for the destruction of the corrupt, degrading, oppressive and inhuman French-imposed system without ridding ourselves of the recognized wrong habits, values and mentalities that we picked up from the system. We have not even begun to live, think and work in the patterns that are required of us by the new society that we intend to build. It is possible that even if we get rid of the present system, we may find ourselves incapable of instituting the complete change that we need because most of us may continue to think, act and live in the ways that the puppet regimes have deformed our minds into doing. In many ways, our words alone have changed without a corresponding change in ourselves. For us to realize our dreams, we are expected to match our change in words with a change in thought patterns and actions. Or else, we would remain our own worst enemies.

A sincere review of the political activities in Cameroon since May 26, 1990, reveals that the movement for change has encountered temporary setbacks in the third phase of the Cameroonian struggle. These setbacks are due to the actions of the anti-nationalists, the pseudo-intellectuals, the unscrupulous politicians, the verminous businesspersons, the oblivious functionaries, the neurotic leaders with a fair degree of intelligence, brilliancy and ruthlessness, as well as the struggling masses suffering from incomprehension. Without clearing our ranks, without being conscious of discipline and enforcing it all the more, without reassessing our commitments and objectives, and without humanizing our dehumanized selves, we may be compelled to wander a little longer in the wilderness of aimlessness, futility and incomprehension. An even when we get to the inevitable change, we may be surprised to find that we are incapable of harnessing our potentials to the fullest because of our old ties to the dehumanizing post-independence mentality and system.

NOVEMBER 24, 1994   *Tchouteu, Janvier*

Chapter Two

AFRICA'S HAUNTED HEART

A specter looms in the lives of every Cameroonian child, man or woman. It is the living president of the land in the middle of Africa, the land that is often referred to as the microcosm of the continent. The specter is President Paul Biya of Cameroon. When rumors spread like wildfire in June 2004 that he had just died, there were widespread scenes of jubilation all across the half a million square kilometer landmass called Cameroon. Days after the circulation of the unverified account, he returned home from abroad where he had been passing his time, intermittently, about six months every year for over two decades, and then declared to the sycophants waiting to receive him at the airport that there would be a …. "Rendez-vous in 20 years' time with those who wish me dead…"

Cameroonians were not the only ones who disbelieved him when he made that pronouncement among other things. Many of those who follow political developments in the world in general, and in Africa and Cameroon in particular, marveled at his audacity. After all, more than 80% of the Cameroonian population loathed his rule; he was already in power for more than two decades as the head of state, after having been the country's prime minister (1972-1982) or the second most powerful person in the system put in place in Cameroon by the French overlords.

But Paul Biya proved everyone wrong. He pulled off another electoral charade and declared himself the winner in the October 2004 presidential election, and then changed his constitution in 2008 that would allow him to run for two more presidential 7-year terms (despite the deaths of 150 protesting Cameroonians caused by his armed forces), meaning that he could be president until the year 2025 (a record of 43 years in power) when he would be 92 years of age.

That explains why by the time Paul Biya held another masquerade called presidential elections in October 2011, he had already successfully humbled the internationally recognized opposition heads (who are all former members of the country's sole political party from 1972-1990, a party Biya has been leading since 1984), promised to give them positions in his government and made it known in plain terms that the system string-controlled by the puppeteer (France) would never allow political change in Cameroon that would curtail France's unrestricted interests in the African country.

The octogenarian Paul Biya is variously described as the Maradona (he fakes and wins elections just like Maradona faked and scored a goal in his "Hand of God" goal) of Cameroonian and African politics, the master of presidential patricide (he devoured his predecessor who passed over power to him, leading to the first Cameroonian president Ahmadou Ahidjo's exile, death and burial abroad—Senegal), the absentee president, the vindictive president, the evil president, etc. etc.

As a German colony from 1884-1916, Kamerun was often referred to by the German Colonial administration and the imperial-minded in the Kaiser's Germany as an "African Pearl", owing to the colony's robust economy, highest literacy rate in the continent in the early 1900s, magnificent physical features, rich and varied vegetation cover, and also owing to its diverse ethnic ethnicities that included all the major language groups in

Africa (Afro-Asia, Niger-Congo-A, Niger-Congo-B or Bantu, and Nilo-Saharan. in fact, historians consider the German colony of Kamerun as a major part of Adolf Hitler's rue over the territories Germany lost after the First World because of the peace terms imposed on it by the victories Allied Powers during the Versailles Conference. As it happens, one of the peace terms imposed on the post-Kaiser Germany was the loss of German Kamerun to Britain and France. That was how Kamerun was partitioned into British Cameroons and French Cameroon.

As a matter of fact, the French Cameroun mandate became France's most valuable assert in Sub-Saharan Africa. Its value was validated even further when the territory became the Launch pad of French General Charles De Gaulle-led Free French Forces that wrestled French Equatorial Africa from the Nazi puppet regime of Vichy France during the Second World War. This force would gallantly fight alongside Allied Forces against Italian and German forces in Libya, Tunisia and the Middle East, before carrying on to Italy and France where their biggest achievement was the liberation of Paris. The fact that French Camerounians played an invaluable role in the war effort to liberate France from Nazi Germany makes the explanation simple as to why French Camerounian soldiers returned home and sought self-government, liberty, democracy, reunification with British Cameroons that would culminate in the independence of the two United Nations Trust Territories. They were merely seeking the rights that they had helped France to regain from Nazi Germany, which is why pundits were not surprised at all.

The formation of the UPC (Union of the Populations of the Camerouns) in French Cameroun in 1946 and the birth of sister union-nationalist (civic-nationalist) parties in British Cameroons highlighted the seriousness of the former Kamerunians to work together to build a "New Cameroon". By 1955, the UPC commanded more than 80% of popular support in French Cameroun.

So pundits considered it foolhardy when the French government issued a decree banning the UPC on July 13, 1955, in French Cameroons, a strategic act that was followed by the party's ban in British Cameroons three years later on the same fabricated charges of inciting violence and for being communists. These coordinated moves by Africa's two foremost colonial masters at the time were supposed to spell disaster for the dream held by Cameroon's leaders. Many Cameroonians saw nothing but duplicity and hypocrisy in the moves, wondering whether the freedom they had assisted the Free French Forces to achieve for France and its citizens was a special right or privilege meant for "White People" only.

When in 1956, the UPC resorted to a partisan war of liberation from French rule, it was a belated move to confront France after failing to resolve the ban in a peaceful manner. That war would end with the defeat of the UPC in 1970, a defeat that came with the assassinations and execution of the party's successive heads in 1958, 1960 and 1971, i.e., the deaths of Ruben Um Nyobe, Dr. Felix Moumie and Ernest Ouandie respectively. It would leave Cameroon entrapped through a French-imposed system rooted in the Colonial Pact France made its puppets sign before allowing their countries to become members of the United Nations Organization by granting these former colonies string-controlled independence.

Despite the period of instability during the country's unsuccessful war of liberation that saw the French Trusteeship masters handing power to those who never asked for or never fought for it (the puppets that constitute the system today), despite the eventual peaceful reunification of British Southern Cameroons with the former French Cameroun,   despite

Cameroon's agricultural recovery and the discovery of oil in the 1970s that saw the country emerge as Africa's eight largest economy and the world's second fastest growing in the early 1980s, Cameroon is today in a horrible shape.

The Cameroonian economy that was expected to grow twenty times over the next thirty years, i.e., from 1982-2012, barely doubled over that period of time. Everything changed for the worse after Paul Biya was handed power in November 1982 by the first French-installed puppet Cameroonian president Ahmadou Ahidjo. Since then, Cameroon has experienced the biggest proportionate embezzlement of state funds ever recorded in Africa. And the country holds the sad record as the country in Africa that has experienced the worst peacetime impoverishment since 1960.

Today, president Paul Biya is presiding over a nation where more than 80% of its physicians are abroad, where more than 90% of its doctorate degree holders are abroad, where Cameroonians invest abroad more than at home, where Cameroonians are voting against the system with their feet; today, Cameroon's neighbors who before envied its high standards of living and saw it as a place of refuge and opportunities, now find Cameroonians envying them as they forge ahead with a sense of direction while Cameroon lags behind in its spiral towards total, complete and horrifying economic, social and political decay.

People unfamiliar with the Cameroonian situation would be wondering why such an abysmal situation persists. Well; the answer is simple. Cameroon finds itself today in a situation like someone in a quicksand because of the anachronistic system put in place by Gaullist France when General Charles De Gaulle returned to power in 1958 and decided to make France's former colonies and territories members of the United Nations

Organization (UNO), while controlling them with transparent or invisible strings this time. French Cameroun and British Southern Cameroons achieved independence and reunification all right, only for the people to find that the new country is quasi-independent under a broader French template of control variously described as FrancAfrique. This French-imposed system has traumatized, demoralized, divided and dehumanized the Cameroonian people over the years.

The Gaullist system put in place by the elites of the French political establishment has as one of its major objectives the exclusion from Cameroon's political power of the union-nationalists advocating for the reunification and independence of the divided territories of the former German Kamerun, civic nationalists who commanded the support of more than 80% of the populations of both territories of British Cameroons and French Cameroun in the 1950s and 1960s. The current system in Cameroon is a partnership of French imperial interest in Africa (economic and political) otherwise known as FrancAfrique and its Cameroonian collaborators (the renegades and anti-union-nationalists who never opposed and who do not object to France's neo-colonial stranglehold of Cameroon).

The system has been effective in infecting the minds of many Cameroonians, reducing them into a state of hopelessness, in a process that lures them to direct their energy not against the Biya regime and the system, but at their neighbors. The system has successfully elevated corruption and the divide-and-rule strategy into an art—it has promoted the notion of settlers and indigenes, it has encouraged ethno-centrism, tribalism, clannishness, regional jingoism, sectarianism and other forms of division. We see a total and complete absence of strategic or even tactical planning when it comes to the economic and social development of the nation. We see a complete absence of social solidarity.

To compound the division and confusion among the people

who reject the Biya regime and the French-imposed system, the so-called opposition leaders these freedom-craving Cameroonians had been looking up to have now been absorbed back into the system, leaving the struggling Cameroonian masses distrustful of politicians in general. Today, the down-trodden Cameroonian people are in a state of political lethargy.

When Paul Biya called for the holding of senate elections in April 2013, eighteen years after his parliament promulgated a law to create one, most Cameroonians thought it would be another charade, as usual. It made no sense for the so-called opposition parties with a semblance of representation in parliament to glorify the charade with their participation. Most Cameroonians knew the system was sustaining these so-called opposition leaders financially and that some of them were in the government, but Cameroonians were not prepared for the extent to which these politicians would go to insult their intelligence. But deals between the ruling party and the opposition were made all right. The electoral masquerade took place and the people saw the ruling party campaigning for the so-called main opposition party (Social Democratic Front—SDF) in some regions of the country, while the SDF in the words of its chairman or president John Fru Ndi "…one good turn deserves another…", openly backed the ruling party, thereby ensuring its victory in other regions of the country.

How could that have happened? Politically-shocked Cameroonians have been asking themselves ever since the open fornication between the ruling party and the so-called opposition political parties in April 2013.

To prevent chaos and ensure a smooth succession, SDF spokes-persons and apologists quip.

"Paul Biya has a deal with the SDF to hand over power to one of its members," some anonymous voices within the SDF echo.

If you ask me, my answer is clear. What was supposed to be a Cameroonian revolution that began on May 26, 1990, became a political comedy played by former members of the French-imposed system or political establishment, a political comedy that has gone full circle. The worldwide wind of change generated by Mikhail Gorbachev's Glasnost and Perestroika that swept away authoritarian systems in Eastern Europe and Africa, and that stirred the vast majority of Cameroonians in the 1990s to risk their lives in the streets demanding political change, was effectively controlled by the system. The desire for change that more than 80% of Cameroonians have has been hijacked by the authoritarian system in Cameroon and the so-called leaders of the opposition. The people got taken for a ride.

The biggest mistake made by Cameroonians was that when the clamor for change began, they followed Cameroonians who had no democratic credentials, people who hardly a year before were in the upper echelons of power in the system, but who at the time claimed they had left the ruling party and now opposed it. All the so-called heads of what the world knows today as the prominent opposition parties in Cameroon (John Fru Ndi of the SDF, Bello Bouba Maigari of the UNDP, Ndam Njoya of the CDU etc.) were members of the ruling party right up to the year 1990, when the system was forced to accept multi-party politics in Cameroon. Like the Pied Piper, these so-called opposition leaders lured freedom-starved Cameroonians into greater despondence and political lethargy. Such a feat was achieved only because Cameroonian liberals, union-nationalists, revolutionaries, democrats and patriots who had always rejected the system, thought these so-called heads of the so-called new opposition, these people who were the first to make the moves to create political parties, shared the vision of the "New Cameroon" that Cameroonians fought, died and voted for, a vision that achieved the land's reunification and independence (though it has never been real because it got usurped by the evil system that today is under the leadership of Paul Biya and his French puppeteers.), but that is yet to realize democracy, freedom, liberalism, progress, justice, equality and development.

False are the statements by members of the compromised opposition that had they not openly embraced the Biya regime and the system, chaos would have ensue in Cameroon incase Biya exited the political scene. There is no truth in the statement because the system in Cameroon is authoritarian, not autocratic.

Authoritarian regimes are usually coated with a sublime idea that could be political (Stalinism/Marxism/Communism, Fascism etc.), that could be religious (Iranian and Taliban theocracy etc.) or that could be an interest arrangement (FrancAfrique). in Cameroon, the system is built around preventing those who believe in the Cameroonian struggle (the union-nationalists, otherwise called the Kamerunists) from attaining power.

The system in Cameroon is a collection of individual interest groups, bringing together the propagators of French neo-colonialism and their Cameroonian collaborators. Paul Biya is the head of the collaborationists. And in many ways, he has been acting over the years as an absentee president. Meanwhile, the state has been functioning zombie-like during his quasi-presence. As a matter of fact, even though the mortifying arrangement suited the interest of the puppeteers and the beneficiaries of the system, it exposed the system to popular uprisings since that means the beneficiaries of the system are not clearly or functionally organized. With the advent of social media, globalization, the maturity of post-independence generations that never benefited from the system; and with the soldiers of the 1990s phase of the struggle dissociating themselves from the so-called opposition leaders, the authoritarian system now finds itself even more vulnerable.

The authoritarian system would be faced by a new political force that never associated itself with the system, a new political force that embodies the spirit of the century old struggle for the "NEW KAMERUN" or "NEW CAMEROON" that confronted German colonial control, stood up to French duplicity in the land in a war that decimated more than half a million of its supporters; the authoritarian system would be faced by a new force that embraces the legacy of those who fought, died and voted for the independence and reunification of Cameroon, a new force that rejects all the values of the system that the French political mafia over Africa put in place in their game plan to control the destiny of Cameroon, a six-decade old evil system that can only lead the country to abyss.

Now, as the open and hidden collaborators of the system openly embrace one another (the ruling party and the so-called heads of the so-called opposition parties) starting with the recent senatorial charade where the so-called principal opposition—the Social Democratic Front (SDF) and the party of Paul Biya— Cameroon People's Democratic Movement (CPDM) supported each other's aspirations in agreed-upon provinces with guaranteed votes from party members, the system is encouraging the creation of elite groups of beneficiaries who see or think that their political and economic survival rests only in a continuation or sustenance of the system. We are observing the evolvement of a system that is shedding any pretense of limited political pluralism; we are observing the entrenchment of a system that openly views the people as its number one enemy. Such a system then becomes autocratic.

In a nutshell, Cameroon's so-called opposition political parties that are in symbiosis with the authoritarian system are aiding the system in its gradual transition into an autocratic system, thereby ensuring its survival in a morphed form. The rapidly changing system needs a strong man to be truly autocratic. This would be someone who has hands on the job to act as the president, someone who the French puppeteers would like to portray as the benevolent despot.

As Egyptian writer Alaa Al Aswany said, "The concept of the benevolent dictator, just like the concepts of the noble thief or the honest whore, is no more than a meaningless fantasy."

It is the place of post-independence Cameroonians to reject whatever farce the system comes up with as change whenever power passes down to the generation after Paul Biya. By absorbing former members of his party who for decades identified with the opposition, Biya is trying to give Cameroonians and the rest of the world the impression that Cameroon's opposition is in sync with his vision for the political evolution of Cameroon. Unfortunately, the system does not intend to let the majority of Cameroonians participate or have a say in Cameroon's political development or evolution.

The New Cameroon will be founded. Not by beneficiaries of the system (past and present) but by those who have always rejected it as an evil system that has been leading Cameroon into abyss.

But then, in founding the New Cameroon, patriotic, honest, democratic, unbiased and progressive minded Cameroonians would have to reconcile a country where:

- the system made sure that most of its historic figures who dedicated their lives and even died for the cause for Cameroon's reunification and independence got killed and buried like dogs at home and abroad,
- the bodies of some of these historic figures that got buried abroad are missing,

- a few of the historic figures who thought they could contribute in nation-building got sidelined, cowed and humiliated by the system,
- its first head of state died and is buried abroad,
- and where the people have been insulted for more than five decades by the regimes of Ahmadou Ahidjo and Paul Biya through an imposed minority system that sowed the seeds of division, corruption, mediocrity, fear and despondence that are haunting Cameroon today.

The ideas and ideals of the New Cameroon hatched by the country's historic civic-nationalists and developed over the years by post-independence union-nationalists is Cameroon's only bargain with the future. It is the only nucleus around which Cameroon can reconcile with its turbulent past; it is the nucleus that all the strata of Cameroonian society can connect to in the process of nation building; it is the only nucleus around which a free, democratic, liberal, fair and prosperous Cameroon can be built. The New Cameroon would lead the country in taking its merited place in the central African region, Africa as a whole, and the world at large. That would be possible only if we confine the legacies of the Ahidjo/Biya regimes and the suffocating French-imposed system to the dustbin of history.

Janvier Tchouteu   06/04/2013

Chapter Three

Politicians and Revolutionaries in the Struggle for the New Cameroon

Politicians are not those who are meant to change a system and take a country out of an impasse into the future. That is the work of revolutionaries.

Politicians operate in established systems and do the job of politicking to defend, safeguard or promote certain interests, be they individual, group, ethnic, regional, linguistic or national, based on empty phrases or through a clearly defined thought formulation (idea or concept).

Revolutionaries on the other hand are those challenging a system, expecting to bring it down and institute a new system that would serve the interest of the trodden majority (the suffering or struggling masses). In the cause to bring down the system, revolutionaries do not expect to benefit or thrive from the struggle. Instead, they are prepared to sacrifice everything for the struggle.

The sad thing is that while the Cameroonian struggle to change the system is a revolutionary struggle, most of the leadership in the so-called opposition parties talk of politics and expected rewards even though they are still engaged in the struggle to change the system. That is why most of them compromised the ideals of the struggle with excuses that "it is impossible to live on clean politics as a genuine opposition in Cameroon." There are and there have been Cameroonians who selflessly gave in their worth to the struggle and felt it was dishonorable to use the struggle to achieve personal benefits. They were and are the union-nationalists and revolutionaries.

During my years of involvement in the struggle, I finally realized that the system (the Ahidjo-Biya regimes backed by the French mafia group controlling African affairs) feared and respected these revolutionaries and union-nationalists for their genuineness, unwavering nature and integrity. But strangely enough, the politicians who profess to be in the opposition conceived a hatred for these revolutionaries and union nationalists just because these revolutionaries and union nationalists are genuine and are not like them, and because they look with horror at the deception of the politicians who are trying to live off politicking and in doing so, compromised the struggle and betrayed the aspirations of the struggling masses.

Strangely enough, we failed in this phase of the struggle (1990-2002) because politicians led the struggle to change the system (a revolutionary demand) instead of revolutionaries and union-nationalists who are far less likely to be compromised by the negative values of the anachronistic French-imposed system.

Janvier Tchouteu   Friday, 15 April 2005

Chapter Four

THE HOPES OF DISMANTLING THE FRENCH-IMPOSED SYSTEM IN CAMEROON, OF NEUTRALIZING THE PARASITIC POLITICAL ESTABLISHMENT AND OF ENDING THE BIYA REGIME

The struggle to dismantle the French-imposed system and the Biya regime is winnable. And this quest for change is a continuation of Cameroon's civic-nationalist struggle that began in the late 1940s, which is broad-based and devoid of illusions. The most any other struggle can achieve is a stalemate (military wise) that in reality would sustain the system even in the absence of Paul Biya, give it some life for a while, even though it would be less effective in governing Cameroon, especially Anglophone Cameroon. Meanwhile, it would be devastation for Anglophone Cameroon.

So any strategy should be geared towards a broad alliance and a link with reality (taking into account Cameroonian and world realities). Unfortunately, world realities are things most Cameroonians, especially the leadership for an independent Anglophone Cameroon, or what was the former West Cameroon, the former British Southern Cameroons and the former German Südwesten Kamerun (to be called Ambazonia) are naive about. I am beginning to see a dawning realization though. German

Kamerun was considered and treated as a conquered territory by the Western powers, and none of them appreciated the Kamerunian civic-nationalist ideal of reunification, much less the audacity to pick up arms against "The Gods".   All of the Western powers conditioned by their dread of the Soviet Union (USSR) and communism, thought Cameroonians leaned towards the East. And they are allies who will always stick together.

The question for Cameroonians dehumanized by the six-decade French-imposed system and the dictatorships of their puppets Ahmadou Ahidjo (Prime Minister from 1958-1960 and president or Head of State from 1960-1982) and Paul Biya (1972-1982 as Prime Minister and 1982- today as president or Head of State) is:

1. How can Cameroonians rebuild the broad-based alliance against the system accomplished in the early 1990s, when civic-nationalists who before had identified with the UPC, joined the SDF and made it a national civic-nationalist party that fully embraced the dream of the "NEW CAMEROON", the "New Cameroon" dream that fueled the UPC struggle against France and its puppet Ahidjo, the "New Cameroon" dream that fired the imaginations of KNDP, OK etc into campaigning and voting for reunification, the civic-nationalist path that continued rejecting the Ahidjo and Biya regimes (The French-imposed system) even after UPC, KNDP, SDF etc. renegades conciliated with the system, making them accomplices as the system

continues leading Cameroon into abyss?

2. How can Cameroonians rebuild that broad-based national alliance that is instinctively Cameroonian and that strives to build the New Cameroon which would take into account the Hopes, Dreams, Reservations, Fears, Concerns, strengths of the different peoples of Cameroon, while heeding the threats (internal and external) confronting our heavily traumatized country, is Cameroon's only bargain with the future?

3. And how do the advocates for change then work together to dismantle the system and build the "New Cameroon" that began in 1910 as a cause led by Martin Paul Samba and Rudolf Douala Manga Bell, a cause that is in its fourth phase after three unsuccessful attempts, all thwarted by foreign powers lording it over Cameroon.

And the sooner those who believe they are equipped to lead realize that, then the better for themselves and Cameroonians. That realization would be a psycho-social advancement very few who claim leadership qualities can ascend to.

Janvier Tchouteu   *May 17,   2018*

Glossary

Adamawa	The southernmost province that was carved out of the former Grand North Province. It is a plateau region.
Akonolinga	A town in the Center Province. It is also the capital of the Nyong and Nfomou Division.
Akum	A Ngemba settlement 9 miles from Bamenda along the Bafoussam-Bamenda road. It is also a traditional Ngemba kingdom and the dialect of the people there.
Ambam	A town in the South Province. It is a sub-divisional capital in Ntem Division.
Ashia	Word used by both English and French speaking Cameroonians to express sympathy, condolence, consolation, encouragement, compassion, harmony, understanding, agreement, thankfulness, and caution.

Bafang

The capital of Upper Nkam Division and a Bamileké kingdom in the West Province.

Bafaw

The principal ethnic group in the area that comprises the Kumba municipality. It is part of the larger Bantu group.

Bafedja

A settlement and Bamileké kingdom in the Nde or Banganté Division, West Province.

Bafoussam

The capital of the West Province and Mifi Division. Also a traditional Bamileké kingdom.

Bafut

A settlement and traditional Ngemba kingdom about 18 miles from Bamenda in the Northwest Province.

Bakweri

The principal ethnic group in the Fako Division, which is located in the Southwest Province. The Bakwerians are Bantu speaking of the Sawabantu subgroup.

Balengou

Bamileké settlement and kingdom in the Nde Division, West Province.

Bali

A Chamba settlement and kingdom about 18 miles north of Bamenda, in the Northwest Province.

Bamena	Bamileké settlement and kingdom in the Nde Division, West Province.
Bambili	A settlement and Ngemba kingdom about 9 miles north of Bamenda in the Northwest Province.
Bambui	A Ngemba settlement and kingdom about 6 miles north of Bamenda in the Northwest Province.
Bamenda	The capital of the Northwest Province and Mezam Division.
Bamendjou	Bamileké settlement and kingdom in the Mifi Division, West Province.
Bami (Bamileké)	Diminutive of Bamileké.
Bamileké (Bami)	The most populous semi-Bantu ethnicity and the principal ethnic group in Cameroon. It is also their mother tongue.
Bamilekéland	The western half of the West Province, with fringes in the Northwest and Southwest Provinces. It comprises five administrative divisions, about ninety traditional kingdoms, and eleven dialectical groupings.
Bamoun	A semi-Bantu ethnicity and one of the principal ethnic groups in Cameroon.

Also their mother tongue.

Bamounland	The Eastern half of the Western province.
Bandekop	A Bamileké settlement and kingdom in Mifi Division, West Province.
Banganté	The largest Bamileké kingdom, the capital of Nde Division, its former name. Found in the West Province.
Bangou	A Bamileké settlement and kingdom in the Upper Nkam Division, West Province.
Bangoua	Bamileké settlement and kingdom in Nde Division, West Province.
Bangoulap	Bamileké settlement and kingdom in Nde Division, West Province.
Bantu	A Large group of Negroid peoples of Central, South, and East Africa that inhabits the forests of the Southwest, Littoral, Center, South, and East Provinces of Cameroon. Also the largest constituent of the Negroid or Black race.
Bassa	The principal ethnic group in the Littoral Province. It is Bantu speaking. Also found in the Center Province of Cameroon.

Batoufam	Bamileké kingdom in the Mifi Division, West Province.
Bawok (Bahouok, Bahouoc)	Bamileké kingdoms speaking the Medumba dialects, found in the West and Northwest Provinces. The principal ones are:

- Bawok-Banganté or Banganté-Bawok is a traditional Bamileké kingdom found in the Banganté subdivision, Nde Division. Much of the kingdom is located in the city of Banganté. Following a series of strives in the early twentieth century, it lost most of its territory to the surrounding Bamileké kingdoms, with its subjects migrating to other areas in Cameroon and even founding new kingdoms.

- Bawok-Bali or Bali-Bawok: An offshoot of the mother kingdom of Bawok-Banganté, founded in 1907 with the help of the friendly Bali-Nyonga kingdom. It is an enclave in the Bali kingdom (*fondom* or kingdom)

Bayangam   Bamileké settlement and kingdom in the
                    Mifi Division, West Province.

Bazou   Bamileké kingdom in Nde Division,
                    West Province.

Beti   Diminutive of Beti-Pahuin. It is also a
                    subdivision of the Beti-Pahuin group of
                    languages and is broken down further
                    into Ewondo, Eton, Bane, Mbida-Mbane
                    and Mvog-Nyenge.

Beti-Pahuin   Diminuted or shortened to Beti, this
                    group of related peoples constitutes the
                    third principal ethnic group in
                    Cameroon. The ethnic homeland of the
                    Beti-Pahuin people is in the Center and
                    South Provinces, with fringes and
                    enclaves in the East Province. They are
                    Bantu-speaking and comprise the
                    following:

- Beti (Ewondo, Bane, Mbida-Mbane, Mvog-Nyenge, and Eton),
- Fang (Fang proper, Ntumu, Mvae, and Okak)
- Bulu (Bulu, Fong, Mvele, Zaman, Yebekanga, Yengono, Yembama, Yelinda, Yesum, and Yekebolo.)

- Smaller tribes or ethnic groups Pahuinised by the Beti-Pahuins such as the Baka, Bamvele, Manguissa, Yekaba, Evuzok, Batchanga (Tsinga), Omvang, Yetude peoples.

Beti-Pahuin people are also indigenous in Equatorial Guinea, Gabon and The Republic of Congo.

Betiland   The Beti-Pahuin speaking regions of Cameroon (stretches from the southern half of the Center Province, to the central and eastern parts of the South Province and extend as fringes into the Eastern province), Equatorial Guinea (Rio Muni), Gabon (the northern half), The Republic of Congo (the northwest), and São Tomé and Príncipe.

Biafra   The short-lived Ibo-dominated state that seceded from Nigeria during the 1966–1970 Nigerian Civil War.

Bota   A suburb of Limbe, Fako Division, Southwest Province.

British Cameroons   The western third of the former German Kamerun that fell under British control following the partition of the German

	colony. It comprised British Northern Cameroons and British Southern Cameroons.
Boumnyebel	A Bassa village in Nyong and Kelle Division, Center Province.
British Northern Cameroons	The Northern half of British Cameroons that voted to unite with Nigeria in 1961, following the controversial United Nations plebiscite in the territory.
British Southern Cameroons	The Southern half of British Cameroons. Became part of the Cameroon Federation in 1961 following a plebiscite that resulted in its reunification with the former French Cameroun. It comprises the Northwest and Southwest Provinces of Cameroon.
Buea	The capital town of the Southwest Province and former capital of German Kamerun.
Bulu	One of the peoples of the Beti-Fang ethnic group with a homeland in the South Province.
Cameroonian Pidgin	Also called Cameroonian Creole or Kamtok, it is the Pidgin English spoken in Cameron. It has five variants.
CENER	(*Center National des Etudes et de*

	Recherché)—Acronym of Cameroon's secret intelligence service (National Center for Studies and Research)—that was changed in 1984 to *Direction Générale de la Recherché Extérieures* (DGRE)—General Directorate for External Research.
Center Province	Central province of Cameroon. Comprises eight divisions.
CNU (Cameroon National Union)	Party formed in 1966 from the merger of the political parties operating in Cameroon. It was headed by first Cameroonian president Ahmadou Ahidjo.
CPDM (Cameroon People's Democratic Movement)	The CNU renamed in 1985.
CU (Cameroon Union)	Party formed by Ahmadou Ahidjo.
Douala	Largest city, economic capital and capital of Wouri division and Littoral Province.
Duala	A Bantu-speaking people of the Sawabantu subgroup, they are the principal ethnic group of the Wouri Division and the Douala area.

East Cameroon

The French speaking federal unit of Cameroon from 1961–72. It was formed from the former French Cameroun.

East Province

The Southeastern half of Cameroon. The East Province has four divisions with Bertoua as its capital.

Eton

One of the peoples of the Beti-Fang ethnic group. Found in the Center Province.

Ewondo

One of the peoples of the Beti-Fang group. Found in the Center Province of Cameroon.

Extreme North

A province in the far North of Cameroon. It comprises six divisions.

Free French Forces

These were French and Francophone fighters who continued fighting the axis powers of Germany, Italy, and Japan, even after France surrendered and signed an armistice agreement with Nazi Germany in June 1940. It was formed by General Charles De Gaulle, who was a member of the French cabinet on an official visit to Britain at the time of the surrender. General Charles De Gaulle strongly opposed French capitulation and the armistice signed by the new regime led by Marshall Petain that created the

Vichy regime in the South of France, thereby allowing the North of the country to be under German occupation. He urged resistance against German control of France and its collaborationist Vichy puppets. The movement drew recruits mostly from the French empire, especially from French Central Africa, of which French Cameroun was the base at the time, under the new governorship of Jacques Philippe LeClerc. Philippe LeClerc led the Free French Forces' first major victory in the war with the capture in 1941 of Kufra, a town in the then Italian colony of Libya. It incorporated forces of the former Vichy regime in the colonies from 1943 and saw its ranks swollen by Frenchmen after the D-Day landing. The Free French Forces achieved their greatest glory with the liberation of Paris in August 1944, led by the French 2nd Armored Division because it had the least number of blacks in its ranks. By the end of the war, The Free French Movement constituted the fourth largest military force in Europe, fighting against the Axis powers. The right wing political parties in France have been dominated by its members and the ideology of its founder called Gaullism.

Fulfulde (Fula, Pulaar, Pular, Peul)	A Sene-Gambian language spoken by the Fulani people.
Fulani (Fulani, Fula, Fellata or Peul)	A mixed Negro-Tuareg people inhabiting the Savannah from Sudan to Sene-Gambia, they comprise three groups namely:
	The Mbororo, Bororo, Burure or Abore who are pastoralists.
	The Fulanin Gida, Ndoowi'en or Magida, who are fully sedentary communities.
	The semi-sedentary Peul people who are agriculturalist and ultimately resume pastoralism, but often form permanent communities.
	Foulanis, Fulanis or Peuls are the second most populous ethnic group in Cameroon. Found mostly in the northern provinces of Adamawa, North and Extreme North. Their language is the lingua franca of this part of Cameroon.
Foumbam	The capital of the Noun Division and the Bamounland. Found in the West Province.
Foumbot	Agricultural settlement in the Noun Division.

French Cameroun	The Eastern two third of the former German Kamerun that fell under the control of the French following the partition of the German colony by Britain and France. It became a French mandatory territory and later trust territory from 1918–1960.
Garoua	The capital of the North Province and Benue Division.
Graffi	Pidgin German word for a grass field. A name often applied collectively to the semi-Bantu peoples of the Northwest and West Provinces of Cameroon.
Graffiland	Cameroonian word for Western High Plateau, Western Highlands, or Bamenda Grassfields. Mountainous grassland region of the Northwest and West Provinces of Cameroon. It comprises the Bamilekéland and Bamounland in the south, and the Ngembaland, Chambaland, and Tikarland in the north.
Ibo	One of the four principal ethnic groups of Nigeria. Found in the southeast.
Idenau	A town in Fako Division, Southwest Province.
Kamveu	The local council of notables among the

	different Bamileké kingdoms.
Koufra (Kufra)	An important but isolated Oasis settlement in the southeastern Libyan desert that was of strategic importance for the North African campaign during the Second World War. Its capture from the Italians by the Free French Forces marked the first major battle won by France in the war, thereby boosting General Charles De Gaulle's prestige and the morale of the demoralized anti-Vichy forces.
Koutaba	A settlement in the Bamounland, Noun Division, West Province. Also a major military and air base in Cameroon,
Kumba	The largest city in the Southwest Province and capital of Meme Division. It is located about 70 miles north of Limbe.
KNDP (Cameroon National Democratic Party)	Nationalist party in British Cameroons. It led the campaign that realized the reunification of British Southern Cameroons with the former French Cameroun.
Limbe	Former Victoria. It is the capital of Fako Division in the Southwest Province.
Littoral	Coastal province of Cameroon. It

	consists of four divisions.
Loum	An agricultural town in the Mungo Division, in the north of the Littoral Province.
Maguida (Magida)	Name erroneously used for the peoples of the Moslem North that originated from the third group of Fulanis—the Fulanin Gida, comprising the fully sedentary Fulani communities.
Mamfe	The capital of Manyu Division in the Southwest Province.
Manjibo	A Bamoun village in the Noun Division.
Mankon	Mankon is a Ngemba kingdom and part of the city of Bamenda.
Maroua	The capital of the Extreme North Province and Diamare Division.
Mayo Tsanaga	A division in the Extreme North Province of Cameroon.
Mayo Tsava	A division in the Extreme North Province of Cameroon.
Mbengwi	The capital of Momo Division in the Northwest Province.

Mboh   A Bantu-speaking people of the Mungo Division in the Littoral Province, with fringes of their homeland in the Southwest and Western provinces.

Mokolo   Capital of Mayo Tsanaga Division.

Molyko   A suburb of Buea in the Southwest Province.

Mora   The capital of Mayo Tsava Division.

Mutengene   A junction town to Limbe, Buea, and Tiko, in Fako Division, Southwest Province.

Nde   Formerly called Banganté Division. It is found in the West Province of Cameroon.

Ngaoundéré   Capital of the Vina Division and Adamawa Province.

Ngemba   The second most populous peoples of the semi-Bantu group. The Ngemba peoples are found in the northern half of the Cameroon Grassland (Western Highlands), mostly in the Mezam and Momo Divisions of the Northwest Province. The Ngemba people related dialects.

Ngembaland   The southwestern part of the Northwest

	Province that is composed of several traditional kingdoms or fondoms speaking closely related dialects.
Nkongsamba	The capital of the Mungo Division of Cameroon. It is also the largest city in the area.
Nkwen	A traditional Ngemba kingdom and part of the city of Bamenda.
North Province	Central of the Grand North Provinces. It comprises four divisions.
Northwest Province	A province from the former Federal unit of West Cameroon and the former territory of British Southern Cameroons. Peopled by semi-Bantu groups of Tikar, Ngemba and Chamba speakers. Their compatriots in the Southwest Province collectively call them 'Graffis'.
Nzui-Mantor	Banganté-Bamileké word for the panther or leopard.
OK (One Cameroon)	An offshoot of the UPC after it was also banned in British Cameroons.
Peul	A French term for Fulani borrowed from the Wolof language.

Semi-Bantu

The unique and unrelated peoples in Africa, comprising the Bamileké, Bamoun, Tikar, Ngemba and Chamba peoples.

Sokolo

A suburb in Limbe, Southwest Province.

South Province

Cameroon's southern coastal province. It comprises the three divisions of Ntem, Ocean and Dja and Lobo.

Southwest Province

Southwestern coastal province of Cameroon. It has four divisions. Formerly a part of British Southern Cameroons and the federal unit of West Cameroon.

Tcholliré

The capital of Rey Bouba Division in the North Province.

Tiko

A coastal town in Fako Division in the Southwest Province.

Tonga

Bamileké settlement and kingdom in the Nde Division, West Province.

Tuareg

A Berber-speaking people of the Mazigh group inhabiting the central Sahara from Southern Algeria and Tripolitania in Libya, to the middle Niger and the northern borders of Nigeria. They moved to the interior of the Sahara Desert to escape the Arab invasion of North Africa in the 7th and 8th century.

UPC (Union of the Populations of the Cameroons)	First national and nationalistic party in Cameroon. The historic UPC was formed in 1948. Banned in 1955, it resorted to an armed struggle that continued well into the late 1960s.
Victoria	Former name of Limbe. Was founded in 1857 by missionaries for the settlement of rescued or freed slaves.
West Province	The southern half of the Western Highlands of Cameroon. It is populated by the Bamileké and Bamoun peoples. It is also Cameroon's cultural and agricultural heartland, and is remembered for its historic role as the center of the country's nationalism and liberation struggle against the French Army in the land. It comprises the six divisions of Bamboutous, Menoua, Mifi, Nde, Noun, and Upper Nkam.
Wolowose	Cameroonian word for a whore.
Wum	The capital of Menchum Division in the Northwest Province.
Yaoundé	Cameroon's second largest city and national capital. Also the capital of the Center Province and Nfoundi Division.